Do You Really See Momma Now

By
Evangelist Madora D. Bond

Divine Invitation

Take a look back at past years of your life. Are you who you were during that point in time? Surely you wouldn't want your mirror to lie, showing you then rather than now!

Do You Really See Momma Now

Copyright © 2024 by Evangelist Madora D. Bond

All Rights Reserved. No part of this publication may be reproduced, stored in a retrieval system, or transmitted, in any form or by any means, electronic, mechanical, photocopying, recording, or otherwise, without the written permission of the author.

Cover design by : Creative Solutionss

Published by : Evangelist Madora D Bond

ISBN (EBook) : 979-8-9914454-1-2

ISBN (Paperback) : 979-8-9914454-2-9

ISBN (Hardcover) : 979-8-9914454-0-5

Other books by the Publisher.

Bye Revealed Essence - Copyright 2018

Rest in Him - Copyright 2022

Dedication

I toyed with sharing this publication with Momma, reluctantly anticipating her response. While sitting with her on an occasion as she was preparing to exit this earthly existence, she looked at me and quietly said "I get it now." I realized the Lord shared this book with her although I had not taken time to do so.

This publication is dedicated to those with an endearing heart, open mind, ears to hear and eyes to see as the Spirit of the Lord guides you to help an aging loved one in need. Your path may be challenged ~ you can meet it. Be encouraged.

> *I can do all things through Christ which strengthened me.* **Phil 4:13**

I pray my Sisters and Brothers extending themselves with compassion shall ever render care in peace.

> *And let the peace of God rule in your hearts, to the which also ye are called in one body; and be ye thankful.* **Col 3:15**

Foreword

No matter the task or challenge, there is a trustworthy dwelling place to rest.

> *He that dwelled in the secret place of the most High shall abide under the shadow of the Almighty. I will say of the LORD,* **He is** *my refuge and my fortress: my God; in him will* **I** *trust.* **Ps 91:1-2**

Preface

*D*O YOU REALLY SEE MOMMA NOW is dedicated to people caring for aging loved ones {a mother in this presentation}. Addressing their life changes and integrating eldercare impacts them tremendously as well as the care giver. Often the gradual changes in one's abilities can awaken a dawning at a particular point in time that things are no longer as they have always been.

Age changes a family member in ways that may ripple changes throughout the household of others. Being content with the current state of life's affairs does not imply happiness. Change signifies a different state of normalcy with continual modifications as you venture forth.

> *Not that I speak in respect of want: for I have learned, in whatsoever state I am **therewith** to be content.* **Phil 4:11**

Do You Really See Momma Now

*H*AVING THEIR HUSBANDS SUCCUMB TO DEATH, Ruth and her sister-in-law Orpah, living with their mother-in-law Naomi looked to her in continuing forth in their life's journey. Naomi's husband succumbed to death first so even she was left to venture forth alone. As you live among family entertaining the various celebratory rituals and customs, you may tend not to notice just how much things have changed as long as everyone remaining continues to uphold their part of the festivities, comings, and goings.

However, the time had come that Naomi needed to advise her daughters-in-law whose husbands, her sons, had died that she was no longer the young mother-in-law they originally met. Time had waned in her body and her husband was no longer among the living either. Things she may have done in times past were just that now - past. Her strength and energy no longer maintained the pace of years gone by. She admonished them:

> *Turn again, my daughters, go your way; for I am too old to have an husband. If I should say, I have hope, if I should have an husband also to night, and should also bear sons; Would ye tarry for them till they were grown? Would ye*

> *stay for them having husbands? nay, my daughters; for it grieveth me much for your sakes that the hand of the* **LORD** *is gone out against me.* **Ruth 1:12-13**

You became accustomed to seeing Momma on a regular basis. Time moved while it yet seemed never to have progressed at all. A change can seem sudden although it gradually unveiled itself.

Momma was still Momma. However, the season of her life changed. It's as if watching a clock. You'll see it move yet not really notice the hand change places incrementally until it is obviously in a new space.

As we live and are able bodied, we should be found doing that which is right and making a righteous contribution. What God has given us the ability to do should be handled with wisdom. This includes recognizing, acknowledging, and honoring limitations as well ~ especially Momma's.

Not only should we recognize her lane, doing that which she is able to do, but we cannot allow ourselves to push beyond her current measure. Just because we're not seeing her as she is now for looking to find what/who she happened to be yesteryear, it does not change what is before us. This is definitely true if Momma was that give all, loving woman that waited on you and took extra special care even when she didn't have to do so.

Momma is still Momma ~ the page in her book changed

Whatsoever thy hand findeth to do, do it *with thy might; for* there is *no work, nor device, nor knowledge, nor wisdom, in the grave, whither thou goest.* **Eccl 9:10**

If the clouds be full of rain, they empty themselves *upon the earth: and if the tree fall toward the south, or toward the north, in the place where the tree falleth, there it shall be.* **Eccl 11:3**

As we live and exhaust our talents, abilities, and strengths, Momma will sometimes go beyond what she should simply because you expect her to do what she used to be able to. She often vainly refuses to let you see things are a bit more than she needs to handle. Sometimes her vanity doesn't let her acknowledge it's a bit much at this point in her life.

Mommas that are used to working and doing do not want to be seen as useless. However, that should never be the frame of mind entertained by them or us. Perhaps we should consider using {or leaning on them} less instead!

But if a man live many years, **and** *rejoice in*

> them all; yet let him remember the days of darkness; for they shall be many. All that cometh is vanity. **Eccl 11:8**

When your days become dark, they can often seem longer. When you're no longer able to do the things you used to do, even if you don't admit it to yourself, your body will often tell on you by imposing an involuntary limitation. Momma's days may become dark, yet we can shine light by not adding to their darkness with unrealistic or unreasonable expectations.

Come back another time ~ Momma's on recess!

Then shall the dust return to the earth as it was: and the spirit shall return unto God who gave it. **Eccl 12:7**

There is an appointed time for each of us. If our love is as strong as we feel Momma's is, we should not find ourselves trying to schedule her time prematurely. Relish the days she has earned to rest and allow us to wait on her instead.

> Let my mouth be filled with thy praise and with thy honour all the day. Cast me not off in the time of old age; forsake me not when my strength faileth. **Ps 71:8-9**

There is never a time or point to be ashamed of depending on God. He is the source of everything! In weakness He is strength. When Momma thought she had command of her own body and mind the evidence clearly illuminated ~ God is yet in control. He is our refuge - at every age.

Momma learned all the more that He never leaves nor forsakes you no matter your state. He knew the end before its beginning and made plans to stay in the midst.

Momma had to make sure she didn't leave Him. She continues to acknowledge Him daily, not merely when she's not up to par but even when she feels good. Nature might abandon your mind and/or body. God yet strengthens the soul.

> *Let **your** conversation **be** without covetousness; **and be** content with such things as ye have: for he hath said, I will never leave thee, nor forsake thee.* **Heb 13:5**

It is important to give Momma her flowers while she can smell and see them. It's equally important to let her know you brought her some yourself. As a vessel of the Lord and one of honour, Momma will teach by precept and example. She'll teach explicitly as well. A praying Momma will thank God all along her pathway for covering and keeping her. She'll be especially prayerful as her frailty is felt and experienced at various levels.

> *Now also when I am old and grayheaded, O God, forsake me not; until I have shewed thy strength unto **this** generation, **and** thy power to everyone **that** is to come.* **Ps 71:18**

Beauty, dexterity, and strength prevail in youthfulness. As

seasoning and time increase aging, generally wisdom should show forth. Strangers sometimes venture in to dwell in such forms as mental or physical illnesses that rob and hinder agility in addition to sound clarity of mind.

> *But if a woman have long hair, it is a glory to her: for her hair is given her for a covering.*
> **1 Cor 11:15**

A godly Momma is a source of strength and a righteous pillar among the family. The Word of God is her foundational guide. Her resource for all things. She exhibits building a foundation and repair of breaches as they arise.

She trains her children by teaching them and young women that have her in view. Boundaries become modified as she ages, as her children age, and as the young women mature that are associated with her. This is to expand or contract to the extent of the abilities each handles or learns based on what she presents. Wisdom seasons her to the degree of knowing when or if apologies are sometimes needed in the mix of aging.

> *The sword without, and terror within, shall destroy both the young man and the virgin, the suckling **also** with the man of gray hairs.*
> **Deu 32:25**

Momma does what is needed and all that she's able to in keeping the enemy at bay. She guards her house from violence encroaching upon her doors. She minimizes the strife that rises within her walls.

Do you really see Momma now as she's aged and can no longer balance everything as easily as she could before? Her influences may diminish. This is not merely because of her age and abilities, but due to those of her household growing older and more independent but impactful by their choices as well.

Momma can still do it ~just differently at times

Cast me not off in the time of old age; forsake me not when my strength faileth. **Ps 71:9**

It can seem that the Lord is not quite on Momma's side. It may seem as though she misspoke when participating in a conversation with a responsive contribution that is totally unrelated. Her response may seem out of turn or out of character or as though she's speaking to someone else entirely. Initially everyone is thrown off guard, not certain if the response was intentional or a signal reflective of a changing mental capacity.

She heard you and is listening; She didn't realize you were talking to her

In the midst of the conversation her comments do not fit. It could even sound out of place to her own ears, so much so that she appears embarrassed by responses given or reactions expressed in the midst of the situation. Be sure not to emphasize what was stated. Gloss beyond it to steer the conversation where it needs to be directed.

> *Doth not the ear try words? and the mouth taste his meat? He removed away the speech of the trusty, and taketh away the understanding of the aged.* **Job 12:11 & 20**

Age and days should season one with wisdom, especially a child of God led by His Spirit. However, not all actions or speech is governed by His Spirit if we aren't careful or our guard has fallen - for whatever reason. We can betray ourselves a number of ways - age, ill health, anger, idolatry, or other weights or sins.

Advanced age does not automatically indicate wise results. Our conversations can betray us. We must learn to speak in believing faith trusting God every step of the way no matter what we see or fail to understand. God gives wisdom as He chooses - everyone needs patience in application.

Even if Momma's conversation or her action is not quite up to par she needs to be entreated with loving kindness and gentleness to guide her onto a more appropriate course. She may even recognize her statements did not quite get expressed as she thought in her mind and appear a bit embarrassed. No effort is needed to make her ashamed neither to allow her to entertain feeling ashamed.

Momma heard you ~she's waiting

for the words to land on understanding

> Great men are not **always** wise: neither do the aged understand judgment. Job 32:9

There is a saying that one should grow old gracefully.

> *The aged women likewise, that **they be** in behaviour as becometh holiness, not false accusers, not given to much wine, teachers of good things; That they may teach the young women to be sober, to love their husbands, to love their children, **To be** discreet, chaste, keepers at home, good, obedient to their own husbands, that the word of God be not blasphemed.* **Titus 2:3-5**

> Now she that is a **widow indeed**, and desolate, trusteth in God, and continueth in supplications and prayers night and day. **1 Tim 5:5**

Momma's continued commitment to abiding in God shows her family how trust and faith keeps you when you can no longer keep yourself. As her family rallies around - not always as needed - God is responding to her faith. There are days no one is near; she'll call out the need and God sends someone to the door. He knows how to answer!

> *And it shall come to pass, that before they call, I will answer; and while they are yet speaking, I will hear.* **Is 65:24**

Ever look at Momma and just see Momma? We don't always recognize Momma no longer has her youthfulness. To us she seems a little older, but so are we. Yet we don't quite see the nimbleness, limberness, agility, spry step, and smooth movement qualities are no longer there.

That gray in her hair doesn't quite register something is yanking on her youth. Perhaps it's years or her child/children. Maybe it's her grasp or lack of grasp on memories.

I enjoyed being able to zip line until the Costa Rican jungle that would be beneath me loomed ahead. Then I realized the picture wasn't quite as it initially appeared. That's how it can seem looking at Momma and envisioning the activeness of yesterday while facing her current inabilities.

I remember while washing dishes, stepping to the side a few feet. The grown-ups were sitting on the back porch talking. All that mother-wit was being exchanged. This lil' sister was soaking it all up! Suddenly a sharp pain reverberated through my temples across my forehead. That was Momma highlighting the fact that back in the day children were to stay out of grown folks' business.

There was an occasion Momma got off work one payday, cashed her paycheck, stopped and did a little shopping before coming home. She rang the doorbell. I came down to help. The bags of groceries were sitting in the lobby, but Momma was nowhere to be seen.

A thug accosted Momma in the doorway, snatched her

purse and ran. He didn't know Momma! She set off to remedy that situation! The thing is, Momma was in a very advanced state of pregnancy that she wouldn't allow to hinder her as she chased after that thug. The police were called. They caught up with Momma a few alleys away.

I couldn't tell you the end of this challenge. I don't remember it. I dare not ask because if Momma had the strength she had back then she'd likely strangle me for telling it at all. How things change!

In younger years children generally envision their parent(s) as able to do just about anything. Shortcomings they tend to overlook. Some they even excuse.

You see, the only thing to douse flames of evil and wickedness is the fruit of the Spirit. One perfect balance of multiple components. Each complementing the other.

> *But the fruit of the Spirit is love, joy, peace, longsuffering, gentleness, goodness, faith, Meekness, temperance: against such there is no law.* **Gal 5:22-23**

Some love mixed with joy laced together by the peace of God can deflate cruel inconsideration. This includes those intentional as well as unintentional. Consider balancing your fruit well where Momma is concerned. Especially so for a real Momma that expended more love than the pains it took birthing you!

A potential benefit of different writers is that you may

likely read of an experience which mirrors one that could have shocked or impacted you in some way. Reading about it deflates some of the shock. You then realize the situation is only new for you ~ for now, but someone crossed that same bridge of shock already.

When you look and in your mind's eye see Momma's regal frame yet behold that presently she's no longer the same, do you see Momma?

When you look past her pains seeing what she was able to do in a way she no longer remains, do you see Momma?

Don't see what she could do, look at what she is now able to.

Believe in the abilities you see. However, recognize that they're retired.

Short term memory ~ because you didn't forget doesn't mean Momma remembers seeing/doing/being told.

Momma may not eat as she should. She knows she should but does not feel up to it. Maybe she just does not want what she has available to eat.

Momma may not be up to cooking. Perhaps today she just is not able to handle the pots the way she used to do. Assuming she can do as she has always done is a misconception on your part. If you consider the fact that our abilities have changed over the years, why not acknowledge that hers have too.

You may reach a point that requires feeding Momma. Do

not be dismayed. There was a time past you had to be fed too.

Her strength wanes due to health declination coupled with lack of eating. It may prompt the need to encourage her to eat, ply her with healthy supplements, and to pester her gently yet strenuously into compliance. Momma might need reminding that a ride in an ambulance for a hospital stay is not the best alternative but not eating could lead her that way.

Momma's retired ~ today

Wars are waged. They do not always happen on an open earthy battlefield. Momma can tell you they happen in your members as well. A fight ensues within your members battling to do what once you could handle with ease.

There may be times your hands no longer move the way you want. Your legs wobble or crumble, betraying you as if finding a direction on their own. Momma might begin to feel foolish without the control she used to have. Formerly bearing a regal stature that is now weakened could make you falter in leaning on the Lord for strength instead of resting in stubborn pride.

> *I remember the days of old; I meditate on all thy works; I muse on the works of thy hands.*
> **Ps 143:5**

> *He teacheth my hands to war, so that a bow of steel is broken by mine arms.* **Ps 18:34**

> *The legs of the lame are not equal: so is a parable in the mouth of fools.* **Prv 26:7**

> *But I see another law in my members, warring against the law of my mind, and bringing me into captivity to the law of sin which is in my members.* **Ro 7:23**

Momma could be lucid most days. She might even call to check on others to find out how they are doing when they come across her mind. Some may no longer call her back because of their inability to understand her sometimes. At times it is not merely the clarity of her conversation but the sensibility of it that does not register properly during a call. They respect her greatly and would never say it to her, but they will let it be known to others.

Often Momma doesn't hear as well. Even if she wears hearing aids there is no guarantee she will always hear well. Maybe she forgot to put them in her ears.

Sometimes the issue will not be hearing alone. Issues can arise from hearing yet not comprehending what is heard. Her understanding seems muddy to her. Perhaps some of us occasionally hear someone say something then have to let the words rest "in the air" momentarily while we truly decipher what was said. If we can have such a moment imagine what it would be like for Momma - knowing that age is gaining on her and trying to carry her health along too!

On occasion, Momma's short-term memory is not as great. If you're not around often you would not notice. Talk about her childhood days and family shenanigans, you'll find an appointment was needed to allow her time to share the details they encompass. Ask about something you just told her ~ earlier today, yesterday, or even as far away as last week, she may not have a clue of what you're discussing. A short while later she might remember ~ might.

It can be frustrating to discover Momma has short term memory lapses. Initially your responsiveness may appear rude or disdainful by your reaction when she responds unknowingly to something you just said or stated not long ago. Your comments and/or actions may seem dismissive until it dawns on you that she previously acknowledged hearing but no longer remembers anything that was said.

Your frustration levels could peak when you recognize Momma's short-term memory does not always lapse. You just cannot tell in advance when it will. When it occurs intermittently, remember to take a breath before responding to give yourself time to remember that it's just in this instance or just this moment. Be patient with yourself too. Rushing is not necessary.

Hard days can be those when you get fussed out {no, not cussed out although it can feel that way} concerning something so little as reminding Momma of something she said that right now she does not remember saying. Understand that it is not you that the fuss is concerning. It's as simple as the frustration of Momma feeling disconnected with her own sense of recall. She may be feeling as though her mind and/or memory is fading. It's a hard thing to feel you have lost some bit of control, especially over yourself.

Some things may be difficult to navigate as Momma ages. Without wealth, it can be extremely difficult to manage Momma's house and your own. As long as she has her mental faculties, strength and the capability to manage herself and her own affairs there is no problem to have her willing and able to live on her own.

As Momma's age progresses and her health digresses it becomes a daunting task convincing her that the choice of living on her own in her own home is no longer wise. Forcing her out of her own home can be overwhelmingly difficult. It may create a disruptively vile atmosphere in which to live during the remainder of her years.

If Momma has a single child, the guilt trip alone can create an ulcerative lifestyle just coping with the fallout. If Momma has several children, she may feel they'll take care of meeting her every need. This can be delusional ~ Momma may not know the outcome to realistically anticipate. She cannot realistically be aware of the choice to do or not to do on the part of each child, especially if any are married.

Perhaps there are siblings or several children Momma should be able to rely on. If they have spouses and/or children, their immediate family may have other limitations or restrictions, including illnesses that preclude/exclude their assistance. Spacing, financial constraints, health, accommodation limitations are merely a few factors that must be considered.

Momma is not sure why no one comes by as often as she prefers. Perhaps she thought there would be a revolving door of company, companions, and family. How is it that she did not anticipate the dark, vast days of long hours alone?

Momma does not fully acknowledge that her children have their own lives to live. Grandchildren/great grandchildren are engulfed in their own world of activities. She feels she's Momma ~ what's the problem? Excuse after excuse may lead her to realize the only thing she can count on is that there will be an excuse - from someone.

Whoever God needs to be there God will have present.

Wealth or no wealth, Momma cannot be sure who will show up until they actually appear. The child/ren she expects may not be the one(s) that show. She'll learn who she can really count on and in what respect.

Please, by no means denigrate or be angry with yourself or anyone that finds themselves unable or unwilling to see Momma now. I remember when helping to provide eldercare for my incapacitated grandparents, one of my uncles seldom came into either of their rooms. He told me that he could not bear to see them in that state. He never realized they could not bear to be seen in that state! However, the option to choose a different state was no longer within their grasp.

Seeing Momma now requires acknowledgement of so many things. If she can't do what she used to be able to you could find out that you might have to. Stand in or cover the gap if necessary. At the very least, assist her or agree that whatever it is no longer presents a required need.

Often, we may feel someone else should step up, step in or just do a bit more. Keep in mind - that is what **you** feel. There is no guaranteed obligation. You can only guarantee what you contribute when you're able to without hindrances or obstacles that might keep you from being able to do so.

Momma's able ~ and waiting for you to take your turn

Your control or dictatorship over others can be restrictively limiting. You cannot necessarily mandate obligating others. Sometimes you cannot control what you believe you control. Remember though ~ God is always in control!

If Momma can be convinced to relinquish her home and move in with you or a sibling or to a senior residential facility, this prompts a different type of adjustment. Maybe Momma can move in with one of her children. Their family dynamics are impacted in a multitude of ways. Financial considerations not only account for costs daily but include costs just to create new special dynamics within their household.

The extent to which daily care, meals and medication provisions are provided are other considerations that are a part of moving in an additional family member. Privacy for the entire family evaporates or undergoes extreme adjustments. Time to minister to Momma's needs and continual efforts to ensure she is taken care of remain very much a part of the adjustment. Resources continue to be impacted on a continual basis by the change as well.

If you're an only child, life can genuinely restrict your work schedule, freedom, expenses, time, and energy when adding in home eldercare. You could start feeling like an octopus trying to cover all your bases simultaneously! You could become overexerted and exhausted just trying to keep up let alone take care of yourself and Momma. You might even begin to overlook yourself in the process.

Home healthcare assistance is another quandary. The type of assistance and extent to which it is available provide constraints that may impact the family or children in innumerable ways. Time and resources for everyone involved may become crucially limited.

You may no longer see Momma now. You may only envision a role reversal of parent and child. Don't you dare get resentful! Remember ~ your day is coming. Time will not be put on hold for you!

> *And we know that all things work together for good to them that love God, to them who are the called according to **his** purpose.* **Ro 8:28**

Whatever encounters you have please understand whoever needs to be there God will have present. Please, by no means denigrate or be angry with yourself if you are unable or unwilling to see Momma now. Sometimes it can be difficult to be in the presence of someone you know yet find them unrecognizable in their current state {forgetting that we all are aging}.

Seeing Momma now requires acknowledging who she is ~ not was. Seeing Momma now requires acceptance on every necessary level. Seeing Momma now requires holding a mirror that might reflect a future version of you that awaits.

Take time now. Take a long hard look. Do you really see Momma now?

For real ~ Do You Really See Momma Now?

References

Scriptures referenced throughout Do You Really See Momma Now are from the King James and/or the Message Version(s) of the Holy Bible.

About the Author

Evangelist Madora D. Bond continually endeavors to learn more about God in Christ Jesus expounding on His Word in ministry, teaching, and outreach. She aspires to continually increase in knowledge and understanding, sharing with all who desire to learn. She has her master's in business and Bachelor of Science Degree in Business Administration.

Other publications/audiobook by Evangelist Bond include:

<u>Bye Revealed Essence</u> - Copyright 2018
<u>Rest in Him</u> - Copyright 2022
<u>Rest in Him by Madora </u> – Webpage

Farewell Blessing

Look intentionally to see the person before you. Their current abilities, or lack thereof, are as real as they were previously. Accept each person for who they are regardless of who you envision them to be.

www.ingramcontent.com/pod-product-compliance
Lightning Source LLC
Chambersburg PA
CBHW071402130526
44581CB00010B/3